Bozaster:

THE Sloth Who Caused a Thunderstorm

by Leo Grant
Illustrated by Mark Damiano

The contents of this work, including, but not limited to, the accuracy of events, people, and places depicted; opinions expressed; permission to use previously published materials included; and any advice given or actions advocated are solely the responsibility of the author, who assumes all liability for said work and indemnifies the publisher against any claims stemming from publication of the work.

All Rights Reserved
Copyright © 2024 by Leo Grant

No part of this book may be reproduced or transmitted, downloaded, distributed, reverse engineered, or stored in or introduced into any information storage and retrieval system, in any form or by any means, including photocopying and recording, whether electronic or mechanical, now known or hereinafter invented without permission in writing from the publisher.

Dorrance Publishing Co
585 Alpha Drive
Pittsburgh, PA 15238
Visit our website at *www.dorrancebookstore.com*

ISBN: 979-8-89027-060-3
eISBN: 979-8-89027-558-5

Illustrated for my
favorite uncle and author.
-Mark Damiano

Do you know who Bozaster is,
Or what he does and where he lives?
He lives in jungles far away,
Where flowers grow and every day
The sunshine and a gentle breeze
Send golden warmth among the trees.

Well, almost evrery day they do.
Great storms may shake the jungle too,
And as we'll see a great disaster
Is sometimes caused by our Bozaster.
At least the monkeys think that's true.
Let's see if you believe it too.

Bozaster is a gentle creature,
A sloth, whose velvet paws do feature
Just three toes each, both front and back.
His tail is gray, his nose is black,
His fur is warm and soft and brown;
He hangs from branches upside-down.

Now isn't that the strangest sight!
He keeps his eyes shut very tight
Because he loves to rest and sleep,
And if he must move he will creep
So slowly that his lazy crawl
Does hardly make him move at all.

Alas! Bozaster is so curious
He made the other creatures furious.
Thay'd ask when they had work to do
How he could sleep the whole day through,
Or why when they would run and jump
He'd only crawl — the lazy lump!

Sometimes they'd stare at him and frown
To see him hanging upside down.
They thought that it must cause him dizziness,
But surely that was not their business.
You see Bozaster, just like you,
Does just what he was meant to do.
And often creatures get upset
Because that's something they forget.

Just like the hawk who drifted by
Bozaster where he used to lie
And screeched at him, "I fly all day
To seek my food and chase away
The other birds who are not faster;
What do you do, lazy Bozaster?"

Bozaster only looked at him
And slowly gave a slothish grin.

And later on a jaguar crept
Beneath the tree where our sloth slept,
"Wake up," she snarled, "and hunt with me;
You mustn't sleep there in a tree.
Your furry body will get thinner
Unless you come and hunt your dinner."

Bozaster yawned as if to say, "I wish that you would go away."

Nearby a group of monkeys too
Began to chatter, "Why don't you
Get up and swing from tree to tree?
Now that's a game that's fun, you see,
And if you don't mind monkey manners,
We'll teach you how to peel bananas."

The sloth he slumbered upside down,
He had no wish to monkey 'round.

Nor did he wish to have a talk
When next he heard a parrot squawk,
"My gorgeous plumes of red and gold
Make me a beauty, I've been told,
More lovely than a cockatoo.
Does anyone admire you?"

The sloth pretended
he'd not heard
The foolish words
of that proud bird.

And when a crafty alligator,
Waddled by a short time later
And grumbled, "Come down from that limb,
We'll go and have a pleasant swim,
And even though I am a stranger,
Trust me — there will be no danger."

Bozaster sighed
and then he snored.
The gator's tricks
he just ignored.

Now you'll agree it wasn't fair
For all the creatures living there
Within the jungle to be nasty.
And you'll agree that when at last he
Grew dismayed and felt quite vexed,
The terrible troubles that came next
Were not the fault of our Bozaster
For he loved peace and not disaster.

But when the sun began to set
And all the creatures we have met
Had gathered by Bozaster's tree
To tease him for his slothful ways,
Bozaster thought their rude displays
were quite enough. He said, "Ahem!"
And slowly turned his back to them.

That's all he did, the gentle fellow,
But in an instant, bright and yellow,
A streak of lightning crossed the sky,
A crash of thunder — my, oh my!
Soon followed it, a terrible sound
That rumbled so it shook the ground.
The sky turned dark as a black cloud
Blocked out the sun, while just as a loud
As the first clap, more thunder rumbled.
The ground still shook and boulders tumbled
Down jungle hillsides as a breeze
Began to swirl among the trees.

The wind grew stronger every minute
Across the jungle, and within it
Coconuts and cocoa beans
Were scattered into smithereens
While terrible rains sent water rushing,
Filling streams till they were gushing.

They gushed until they overflowed,
And when the lightning flashed it showed
The floods poured over canyon walls,
Creating roaring waterfalls.
The jungle that was once delightful
Was filled with sights and noises frightful.

35

Of course the creatures by the tree
Were just as shocked as they could be.
For all that lightning, rain and thunder
Frightened them and made them wonder
What to do. While some just shook,
And others trembled, Bozaster's look
Was one of slothful satisfaction;
He slept — inclined towards rest, not action.

37

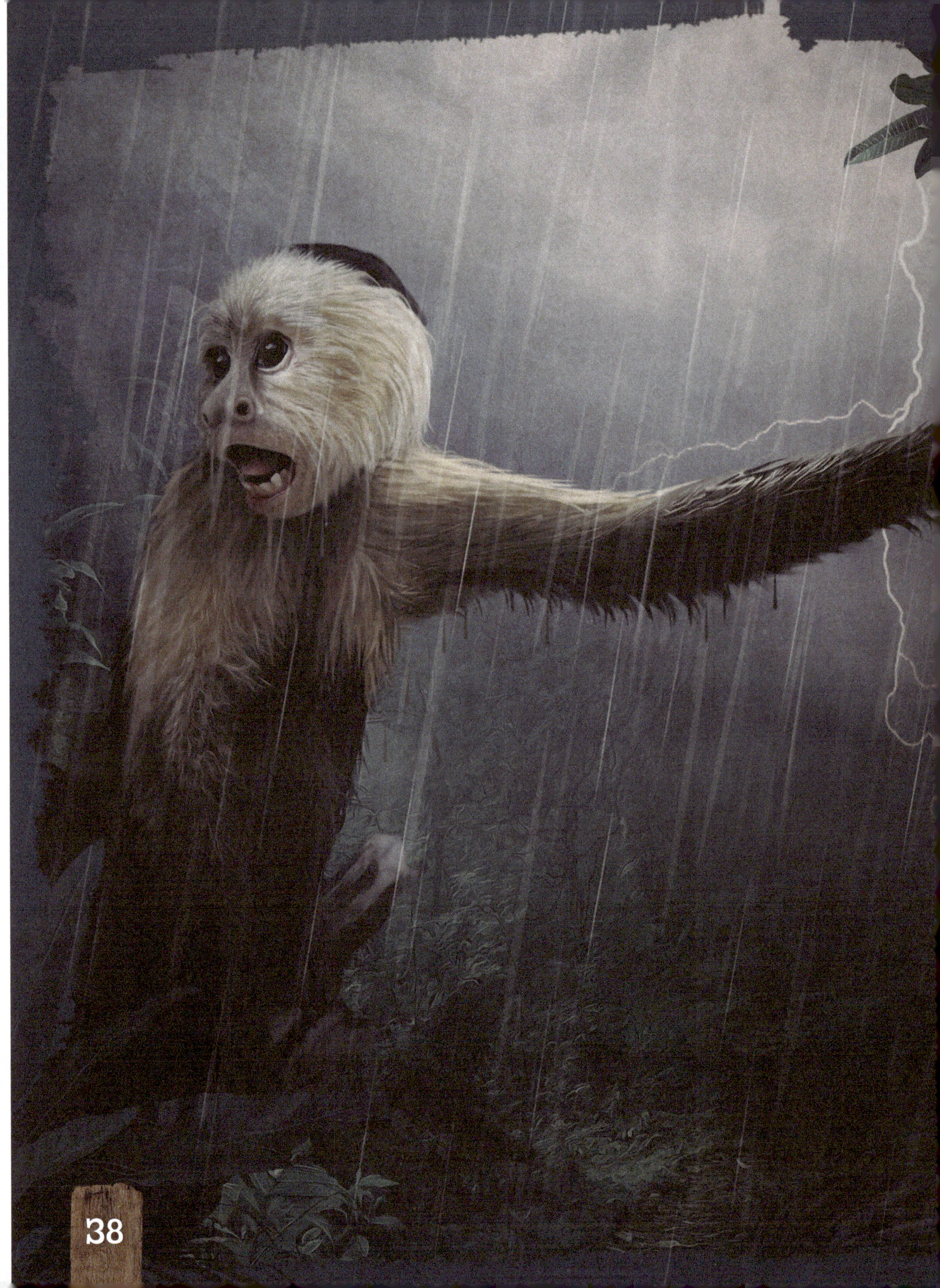

To see him sleeping without fear
Amazed the monkeys who were near,
For they were filled with terrible dread
And wished that they were safe instead.
Then one screeched something that was frightening;
"Bozaster's caused the storm and lightning,
The flooding and the thunder too;
You all can see that this is true."

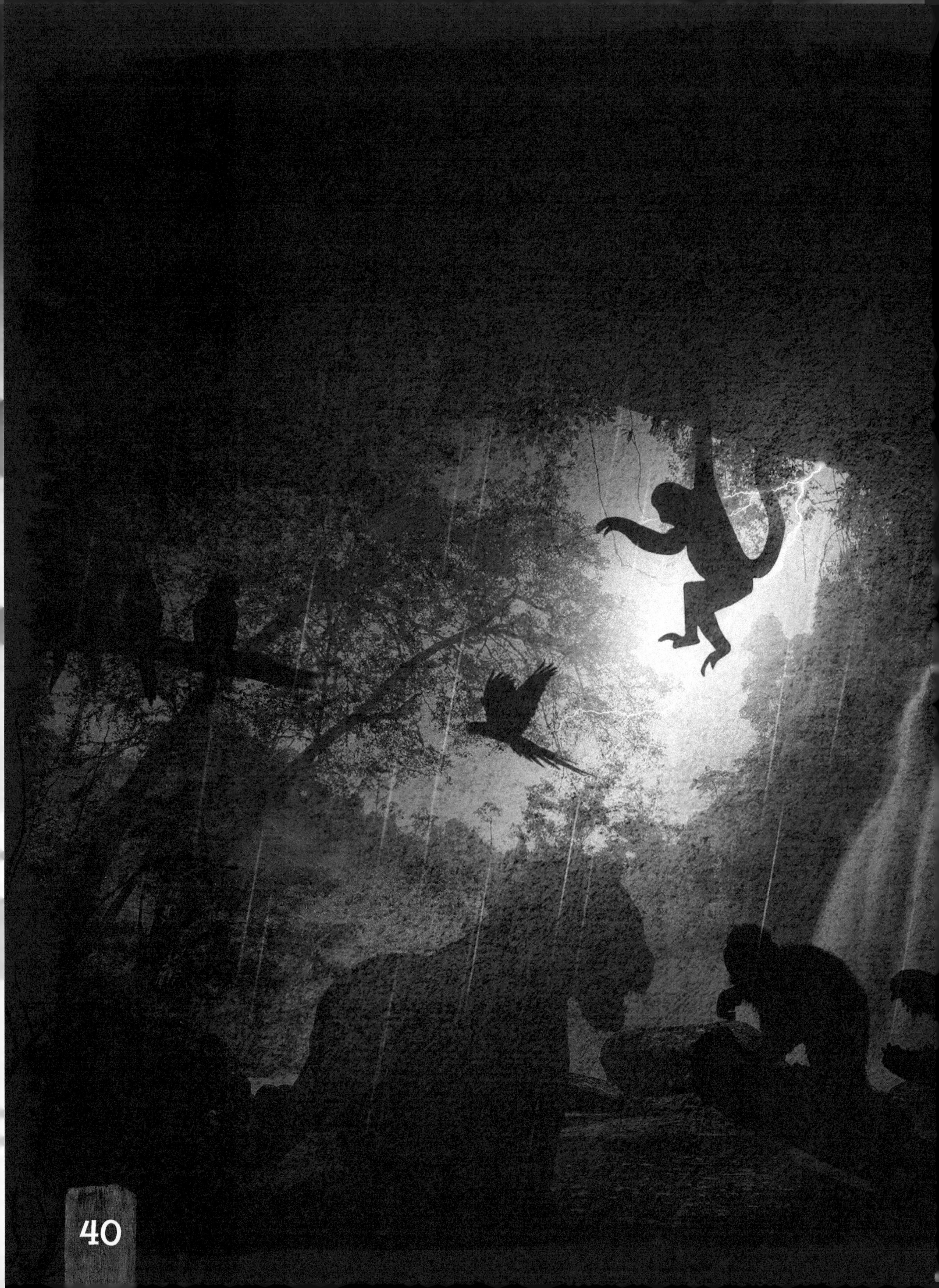

Now they believed what he had said,
So through the jungle they soon fled
And hid themselves within a cave
Where they decided to behave
When next they met our furry friend.
Oh, how they wished the storm would end!

The hawk could only hop around,
For when he tried to fly he found
The stormy winds were much too strong
To let him fly for very long.

The jaguar also feared to stay,
With blushing face she crept away.
In shame she found a place to hide,
She was so very terrified.

The alligator, scared to stay,
Crawled through the grass to slip away,
And with a most embarrassed look
He plunged into a nearby brook.

The parrot who had been so proud
Was so ashamed she cried outloud –
The winds had ruffled every feather
And raindrops made them stick together.

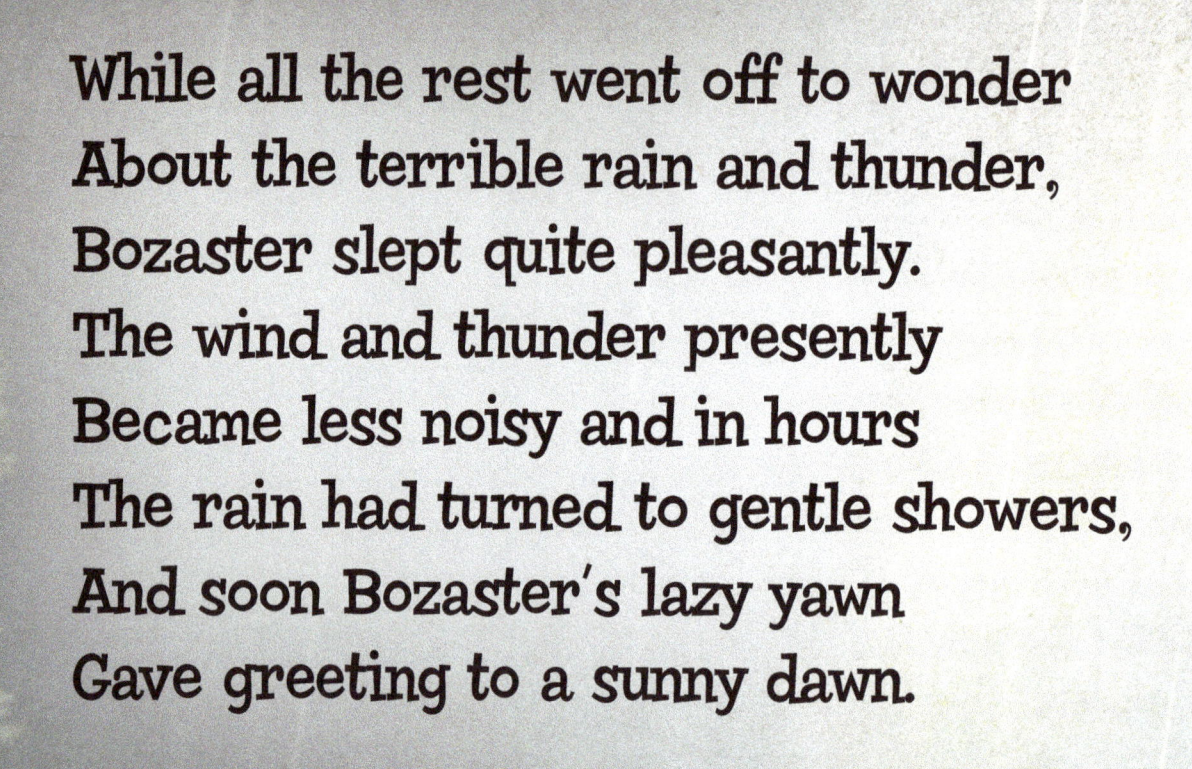

While all the rest went off to wonder
About the terrible rain and thunder,
Bozaster slept quite pleasantly.
The wind and thunder presently
Became less noisy and in hours
The rain had turned to gentle showers,
And soon Bozaster's lazy yawn
Gave greeting to a sunny dawn.

47

The sunshine and a gentle breeze
Sent golden warmth among the trees
As all the jungle creatures crept
Back to the place where our sloth slept,
But now they came — as you'd expect —
To offer greetings of respect.

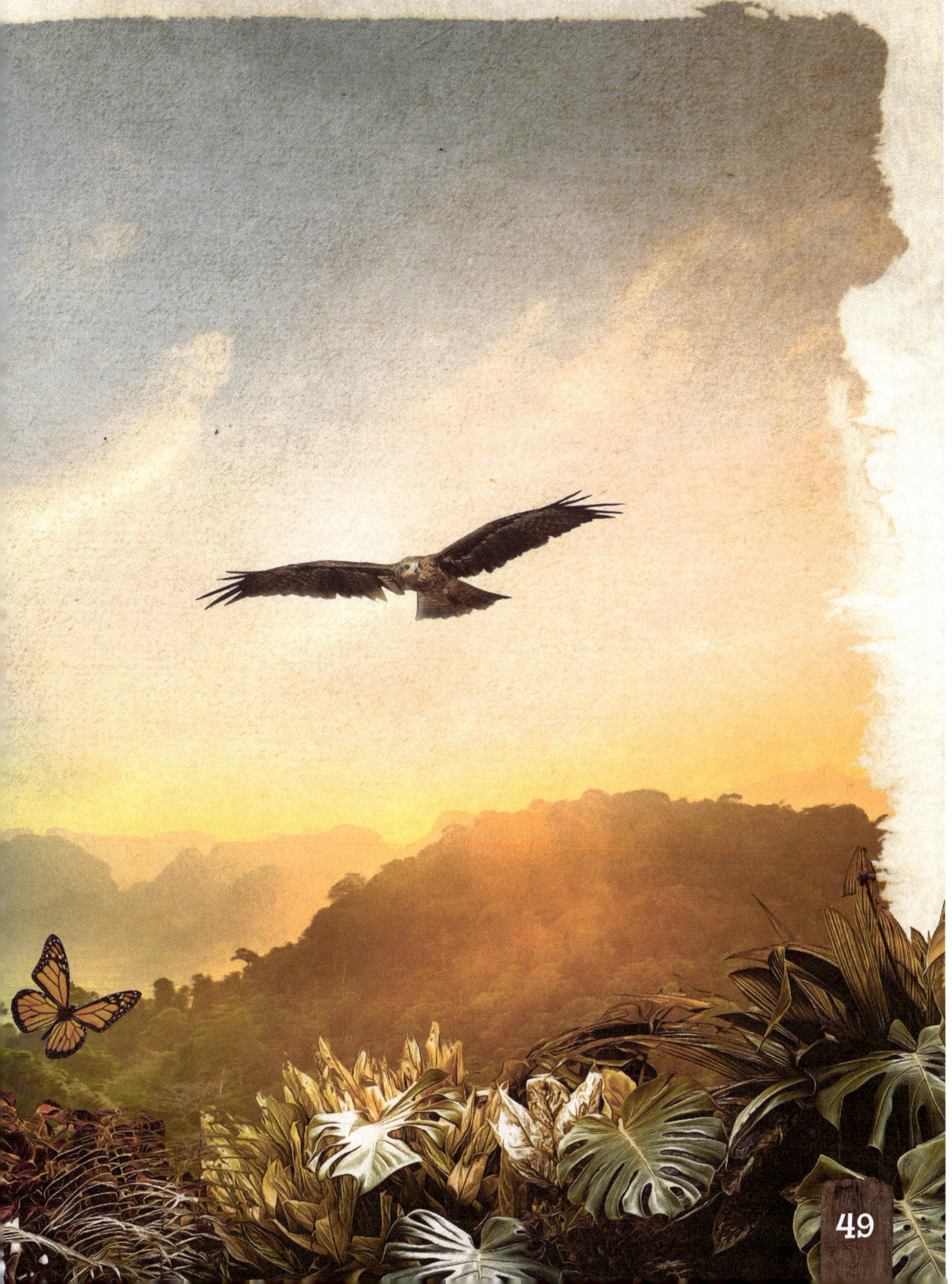

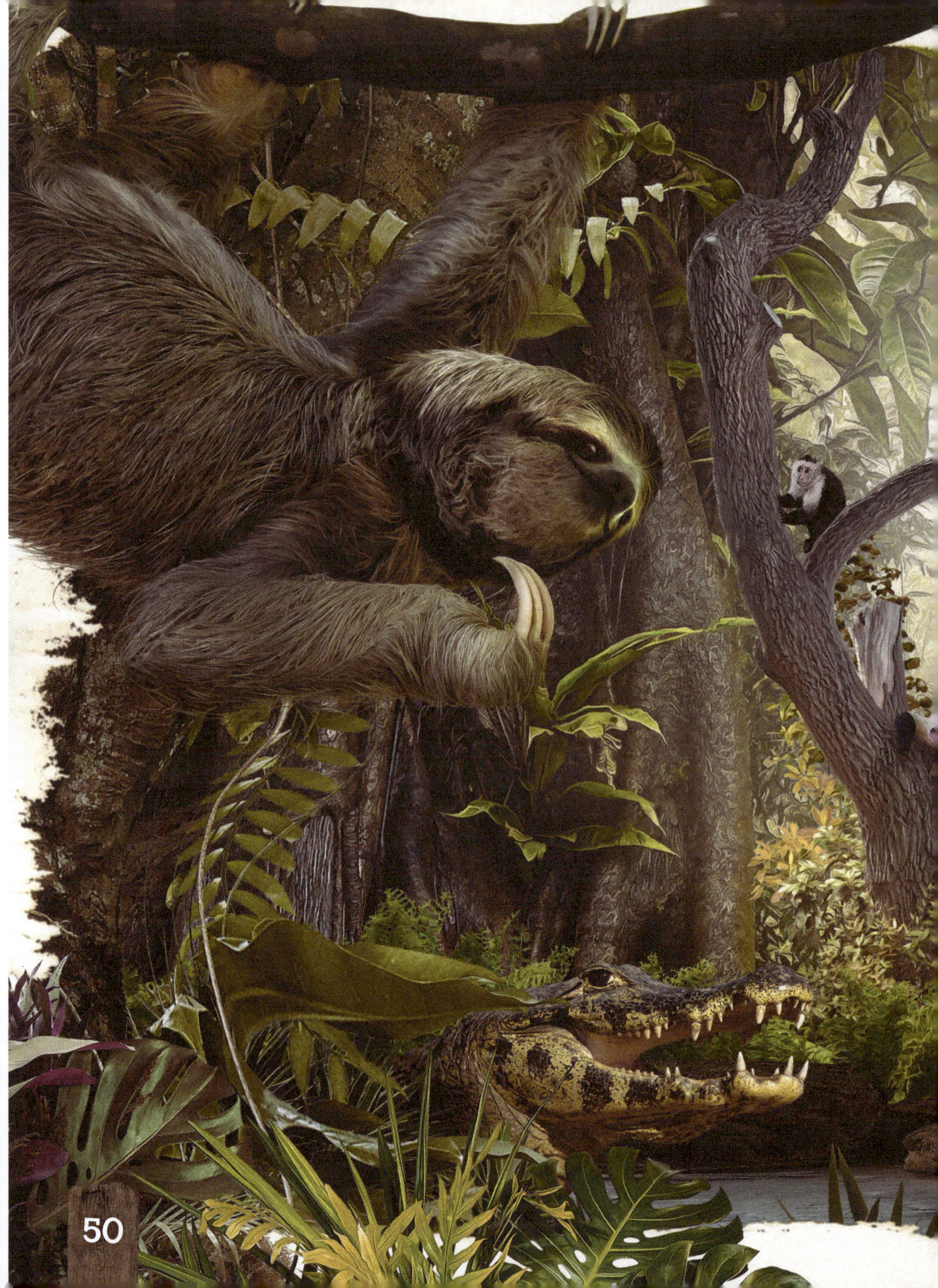

For they were sure that our Bozaster
Had caused the earlier disaster.
They called him "Sir" and said "Good day"
And acted in a friendly way.
There were not any frowns from them,
For now they all respected him.

Our sloth whose eyes were open now
Crawled slowly out along his bough
To find another resting-place.
From the expression on his face
It was quite clear he was amused
To think how they had been confused.

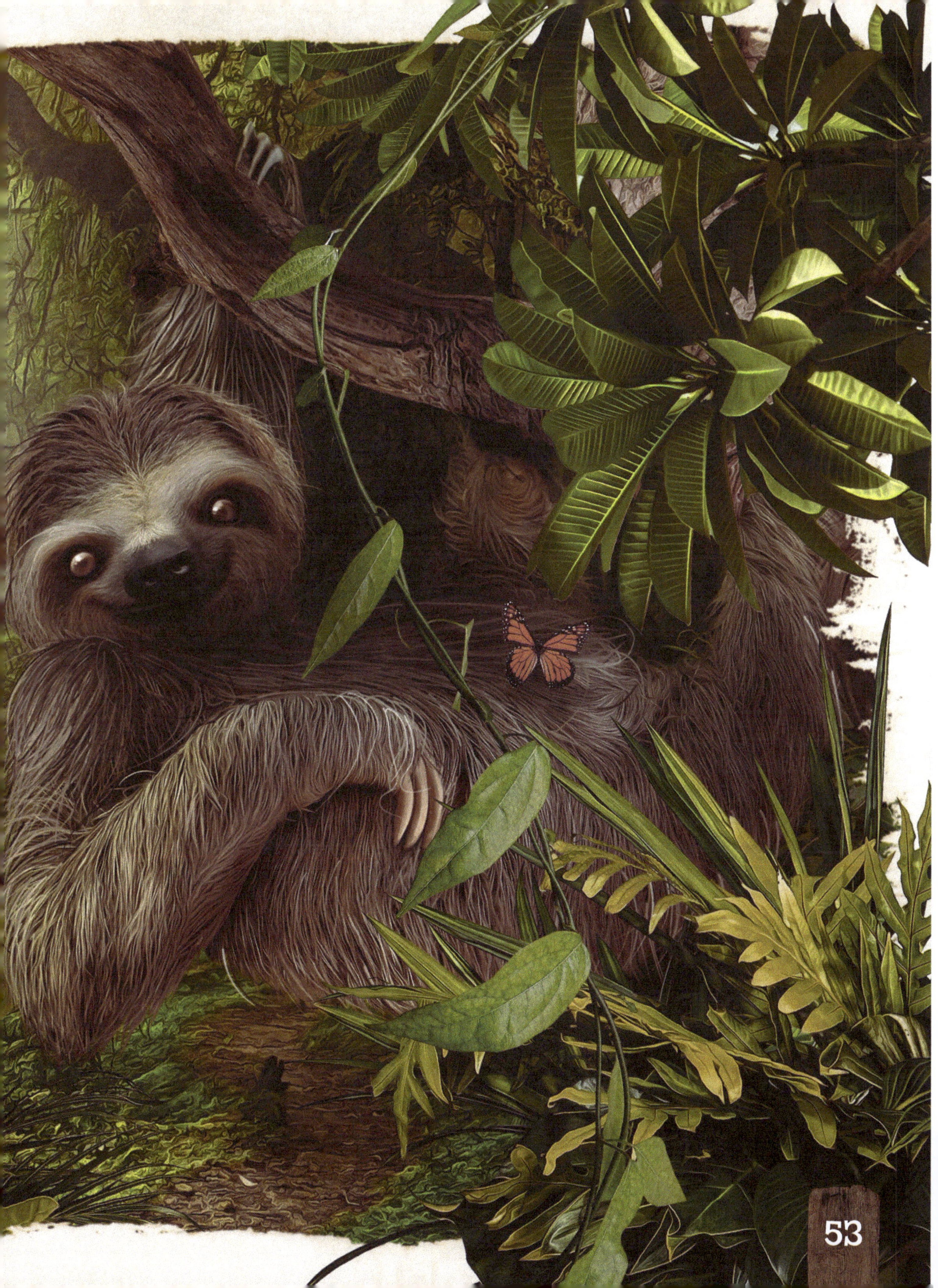

He smiled and thought it very strange
That they should think that he could change
The weather with his gentle ways
When he was resting nights and days.
You see Bozaster, just like you,
Does just what he was meant to do.

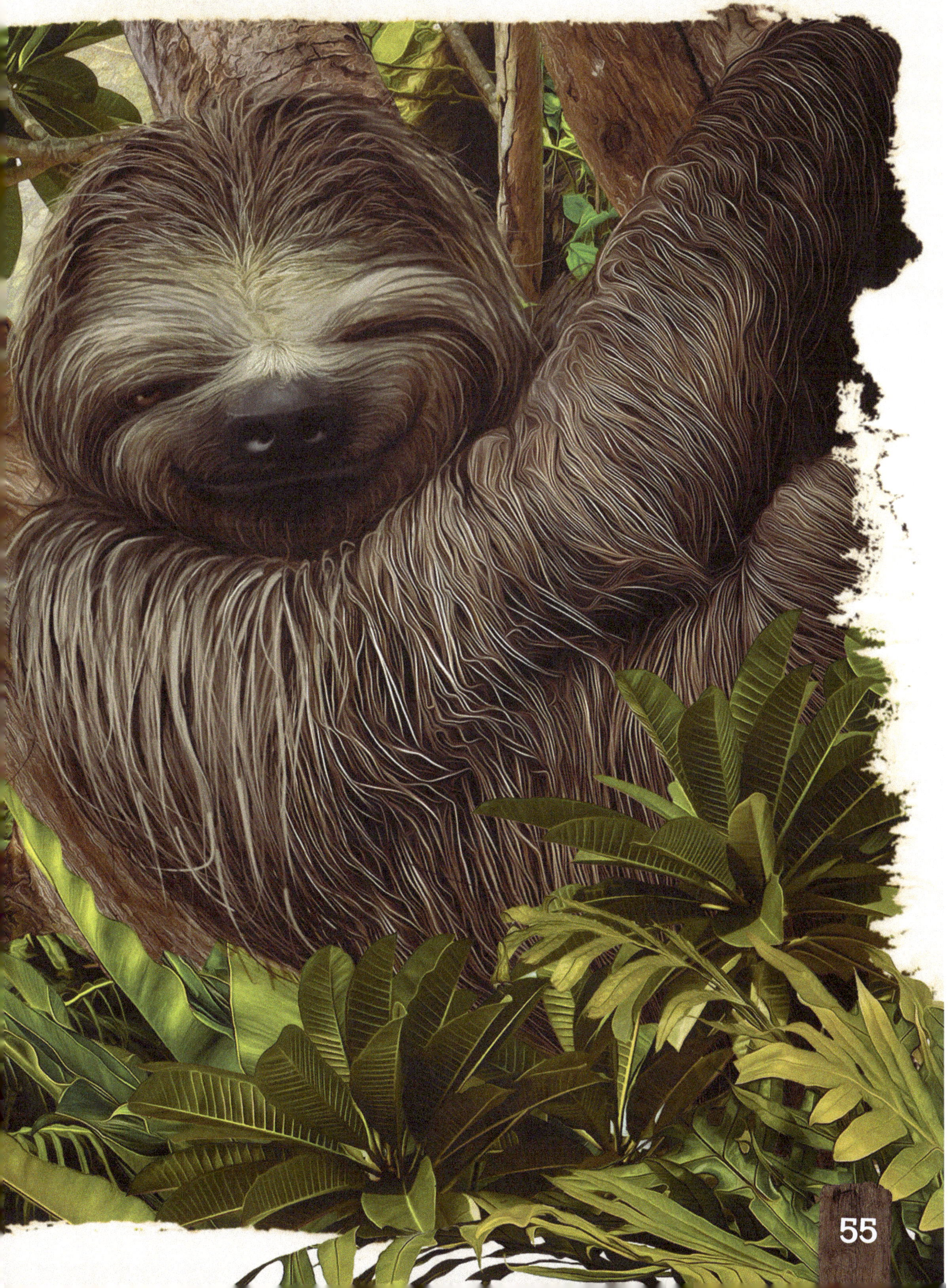

And other creatures get upset
Because that's something they forget.
And that's the very reason why
The animals who wandered by
Were victims of a strange delusion
That caused both wonder and confusion.

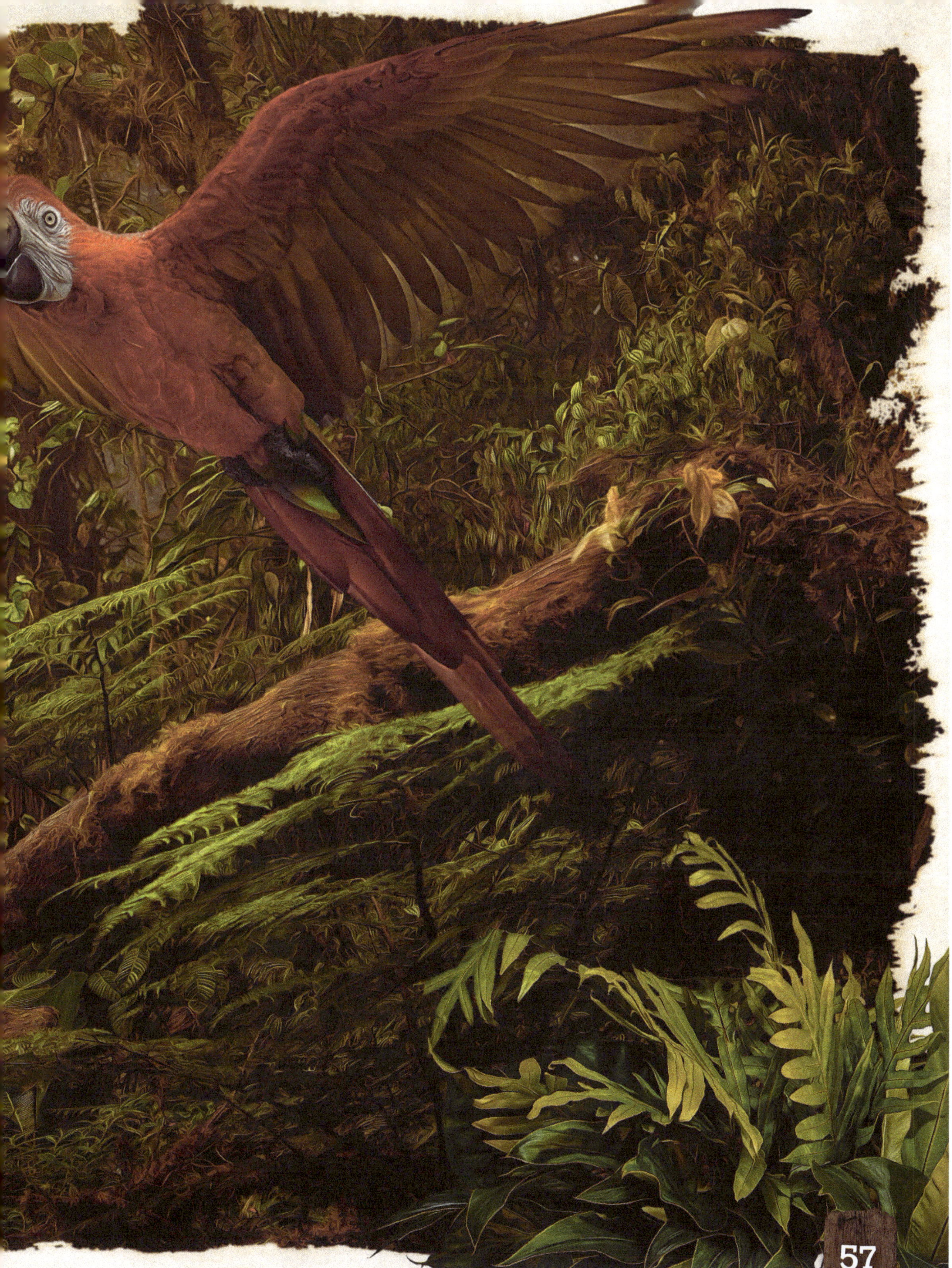

58

Now while he rests and sleeps and snores,
The other creatures he ignores
Believe that he has special powers
To cause great storms and thundershowers.
The monkeys think that this is true.
And you? Do you believe it too?

The

End

Printed in the USA
CPSIA information can be obtained
at www.ICGtesting.com
LVHW071132121124
796389LV00018B/290